NONNO NANNI
IN THE USA

Analysis of the American market

Mauro Tommaso De Candia

INDEX

INTRODUCTION

According to "Plantscope", in the world are produced 200 million cheeses a year. The United States are the world first cheese producer but it is only made for their internal market. Americans do not export their cheese. However, French are the first exporter of cheese in value while Germans are the first exporter of cheese in quantity.

Therefore, here is the issue, USA produces a big quantity of cheese but it is possible to import a foreign cheese in the USA. Are there any massive social-cultural barriers? Many issues are at stake. Concerning the idea to offer a cheese in a new market. Do Americans like foreign cheese? Do they want to import the foreign cheese? Can Latteria Montello export the "Stracchino", a typical Italian cheese?

Americans have increased by 50% their consumption of cheese over the last 10 years. The cheese in the USA has become a true show. For example, the "Cheese mongers competition" in New York, where the best cheese mongers are in competition to offer the best cheese. There are different nationalities and they present the best expertise and quality about cheeses. Cheese became a phenomenon In the United States.

About Italian cheese, mozzarella is the United States favorite cheese. It is represent 1/3 of American cheese consumption (they use it mostly for pizzas or sometimes for hamburgers).

Nowadays, Americans want to discover different food and they are looking for quality. Americans are changed their foods habits as they increase the consumption of ethnic foods. According to Americans, European products represent these ethical foods. The contact with ethic foods comes by trips, books or visits. Therefore, an extensive supply creates an extensive demand. Moreover, Americans have increased their consumption of wine. As such, we observe an increase of "wine and cheese" tastings, which allows presenting news tastes for foods hobbyists.

The learning process is allowed by restaurant or TV show. Restaurants play an increasingly important role in the cheese discovery. The chefs are the pillars of the trend because they are permanently looking for new products new concepts. Americans love to follow the new trend concepts.

One the other hand, Americans want to cook less and less. Nevertheless, Americans want to eat healthy food but quickly with little portion because they do not want to take the time to eat or cook. Many producers have understood the demand and they produce individual cheese part and consumers can eat quickly and easily their cheese. Moreover, the small portion replaced the big portion or the traditional principle "Breakfast, lunch and dinner"; cheese producer can try to found a new principle to eat the cheese.

According to the American website "Statista", in 2014, the total consumption of cheese per capita in the US is equal to 33.5 pounds, which represents 15.2kg. Furthermore, the consumption of Italian cheese per capita in the US is equal to 14.93 pounds, which represents around 6.7kg. If we make the relation, it means that Americans consumed 44% of Italian cheese among all the cheese they are eating per year. Thanks to these statistics, we can say that Americans will be open to taste a new kind of cheese if it comes from Italy. Because as we know, the Italian culture and food is already renown in America. Italy is famous for its quality products and especially for cheese. Americans are huge consumers of products derivative from the Italian cuisine (pizza, pasta...), so if we offer a product with a deep Italian culture (a company with a family background, tradition, taste...) they will trust the company and be able to buy the product.

Stracchino can be proposed in different dishes (for example pizza, cheesecakes or pasta). A good point, Stracchino can be used inside the pizza (knowing that American like and eat pizza). Stracchino can replace mozzarella for example (favorite American cheese).

I got in touch with an American chef based in Milan to meet her and see how she could mix Stracchino with the American cuisine. Unfortunately, I could not meet her directly and test her recipes but she gave me her recipes ideas, how she would have incorporated Stracchino in her dishes. For her Stracchino can be used as a substitute of Philadelphia (cream cheese). Here are some of her suggestions:

-used to replace Philadelphia in cooking like pasta with zucchini to add a creamy-ness;

-with smoked salmon and rocked salad on crackers;

-as appetizers: With chives, black pepper and a little oil mixed in with stracchino and served as dip with assorted crackers or raw vegetables.

These are ideas of recipes that can fit with the American cuisine and Italians products.

Target market in the US: Italian immigrants that might want something from home. Younger generations that want a quick snack, mothers of young children. Can target the health food market because it is also lower in calories because they are also making a probiotic stracchino.

INTERVIEW TO AMERICAN STUDENTS

To make sure that the product will satisfy Americans' tastes, I decided to interview a few American Erasmus students who can also represent the younger generations mentioned above. First I asked them questions about Italy in general, which cheese represent for them Italy. They all answered parmesan and mozzarella. Then, I asked them, how often and when they prefer to eat cheese. They said that they eat cheese a lot, they eat it as a snack, to mix with different dishes so for lunch or dinner, and one of them even said that she is eating cheese for breakfast. After these questions, I made them taste stracchino on fresh bread with a piece of Parma ham. Their first reaction was positive; they really loved it at first bite. So after I asked them if it will be possible for them to eat stracchino and they said: "yes of course, and it looks like cream cheese but it's fresher than cream cheese". For them stracchino represents a fresher, healthier and "fancy" cheese compared to the American's one. To understand better what the expectations of the American consumer are, we also asked them with what and how they will eat stracchino. They suggested cooking it with pasta, for cheesecake, salad or just with bread like that.

I also wanted to know how they usually buy cheese, if they take care about the origin of the product, the quality or the brand for example. They said that most of the time they only consider the brand. As Nonno Nanni is not present now in the US, the brand will have to focus really on advertising. The brand should do a strong advertising campaign on TV because Americans watch TV a lot. It will the best way for them to be known and to show how and with what the product can be eaten, because for the moment they have totally no idea of how to use it.

When I said the word "cheese" to them, what comes straight to their mind are "cheeseburger", "macaroni cheese" or "slice cheese". Stracchino has a good potential to enter this market because it is very different and not present, it will change the American way of eating cheese but in a fresher and healthier way. In addition, this is what most of American people are looking for now.

At the end of the interview, they even asked me where they could buy stracchino so it means that they were really convinced by the product. Therefore, for Nonno Nanni it is encouraging for them to know that stracchino's taste can appeal to American people.

COMMUNICATION
AND ADVERTISING

The National Dairy Council has started up a campaign about dairy products (three a day program). It wanted to promote the dairy products. On the other hand, the United States are increased the immigrant people and it can explain the number of exotic products in the supermarket. Moreover, the Spanish and Italian cheeses have researched in the supermarket and the delicatessen by the consumers. Therefore, the cheese market must answer at this new market.

For the communication, the advertising must present the Italian lifestyle or the typical Italian. It is necessary that consumers feel the part of Italy when they buy the cheese. First, the cheese had an Italian name, so it is difficult to change the cheese environment. The TV advertisement must display a part of Italy with the family values, togetherness and craft. Second, the product must be to present by small portion, the product must be easy to use. For example, Americans want to prepare a sandwich or pizza, it is necessary that the product is small, easy to use and the packaging shows a part of Italy (with the color of flag for example). In addition, of the brand name "Nonno Nanni" and the product's name "Stracchino", they should also write in small English a few words about what kind of cheese it is because as it is new for Americans and not present on the actual Italian's packaging. For example, they could write "Fresh creamy cheese" or "fresh milk-based cheese" under "Nonno Nanni".

Concerning the TV advertising, the brand should also show how the product could be used. Because as the Americans students told me, for the moment American people have no idea of this kind of cheese and how to eat it. In the TV ad, Nonno Nanni should show cooking ideas or people eating this cheese with bread to give the envy to American consumers to buy it.

One the other hand, the communication does not pass only by the advertising or packaging but with the direct marketing. For example, Nonno Nanni can propose to test, to show the cheese in the supermarket, and to propose the cooking tips (always with the idea that the cooking time is short). The moment must be fast but at the same time friendly. The customer has to want to test afterward at his home; it is necessary to keep an element of mystery.

PEST ANALYSIS

P EST analysis is required before to elaborate a possible market strategy. It defines different external factors, which can affect, in a positive or in a negative way, our business.

A – Political factors

- FDA (Food and Drug Administration) and USDA (American agriculture department) regulations: they limit the standardization of products by imposing some restricted policies. Our product could not respect specific alimentary certifications required of the basic components (such as milk).
- Annual import quotas: they set a specific quantity to be sold in the local market. We should get the import permissions.
- Economic recovery: the local government provides economic growth through expansive public policies, which are aimed to guarantee an increment in the consumption and a possible recover from the recent crisis.

B – Economical factors

If the market is facing a growth phase and there is a demand expansion, it could be easier for Nonno Nanni to introduce their product.

- Unemployment rate: a low unemployment rate affects consumptions in general.

- €/$ exchange rate: it allows to apply different price strategies.

C – Social factors

They are relevant to define a better market segmentation and to find out possible market niches. Nonno Nanni healthy product is relied to a long tradition and the quality is their first priority. I need to define a responsible family of consumers.

- Education: graduated people are willing to be more concerned about a healthy and correct alimentation.
- Mass consume: it represents an important obstacle to our business. Many consumers do not take care about an equilibrate diet, even worse mass consumption is able to dictate a sort of lifestyle.
- Green production: today there are more people who are concerned about the environment and they prefer a bio production. We can connect our qualitative message to a responsible production.

D – Technological factors

- Research and development: new technologic discoveries help to face different realities and to find more solutions.

SWOT ANALYSIS

STRENGHTS	WEAKNESSES
Exchange rate	Low ecological production
Economic recovery	Product quality
OPPORTUNITIES	THREASTS
Lower unemployment rate	Food regulations

After the PEST Analysis, the next major concern is to distinguish all the relevant factors I found and divide them into 4 main categories. This phase is realized by using a SWOT Analysis. Each single factor can have a positive or negative impact. This evaluation allows us to define possible solutions, advices and ideas for our business.

I consider the exchange rate as a strength because today is 1€ = 1.05 USD around and the Dollar's power still remains strong, this is an incentive to operate in this market.

A positive new is the US economy is moving through a quicker recovery and customers are willing to reduce their savings and to spend more.

When I talk about weaknesses a relevant obstacle Nonno Nanni has to face is a low green production together with the quality of the products used. Even if there are some green productions, the gap between Italy and the States remains wide, not many companies adopt this technique and this fact can seriously limit the commercialization of our cheese.

Furthermore, there are some regulations that can limit the importations of Nonno Nanni products.

A favorable factor is the unemployment rate, which is 5.6% (December 2014) compared to the 10% in Europe.

I want to take in consideration the education level in the US (41% 25-34 years, 16th in the world rank) because it allows me to define a more responsible population who prefer to consume good qualitative products.

NEW YORK STATE

T he United States of America has a size similar to the European Union, so we suggest beginning to penetrate the American market in the State of New York because it is located on the east coast and well connected with Italy.

New York State has a population of 19 million inhabitants, of which 14.4% are Italian-Americans.

New York City is well linked to Italy via the international airport John F. Kennedy with Milan Malpensa airport. Several airlines offer the service of cargo flight between Milan and New York, including Cargolux and Emirates Sky Cargo. The target price for a transport of 100 kg of product with cargo flight between Milan and New York is about 300 €. The price is subject to change, depending on the airline company, the volume and type of goods transported.

First, we want to know who the main cheese producers in the State of New York. Below the list.

- **Coach Farm Enterprises, Inc.**
  105 Mill Hill Road
  Pine Plains, NY 12567
  United States
  Phone: (914) 241-2300
  Web Site: http://www.coachfarm.com
  Coach Farm produces goat cheese artisan such as those that

were once only in the remote villages of France. The company has over 900 French Alpine dairy goats. The dairy where they produce the cheese is directly connected to the milking parlor.

These cheeses are high quality and are sold in specialty stores and luxury restaurants.

- **Lactalis Deli**

77 Water St, Mezzanine Level

New York, NY 10005

United States

Phone: (503) 699-3144

Web Site: http://www.presidentcheese.com

Groupe Lactalis is present in the State of New York with French cheeses Président. Number 1 French Brie.

- **Meadowood Farms**

5157 Ridge Road

Cazenovia, NY 13035

United States

Phone: (315) 655-0623

Web Site: http://www.meadowoodfarms.com

Meadowood Farms expands on a plot of 225 acres in Madison County, New York.

Farmstead cheeses are produced from sheep grazing raised East Friesian sheep.

It breeds excellent Registered Belted Galloway beef cattle.

- **Old Chatham Sheepherding Company, Inc.**

155 Shaker Museum Road

Old Chatham, NY 12136

United States

Phone (518) 794-7733

Web Site: http://www.blacksheepcheese.com

The sheep cheese of Old Chatham Sheepherding is produced in the Hudson Valley of New York. The logo Black Sheep on green packaging is easy to spot. The cheese and yogurt can be found in many specialized markets and gourmet shops, or you can order directly from the website.

• **Yancey's Fancy, Inc.**

857 Main Rd.

Corfu, NY 14036

United States

Phone: (585) 599-4448

Web Site: http://www.yanceysfancy.com

The company has updated and redesigned its website YanceysFancy.com.

The cheeses are handmade using special polymerization techniques developed to emphasize the taste that is no longer commercially available in the type's cheddar from most of the big producers of cheese today. Yancey's Fancy is the largest producer of fresh ricotta on the east coast. The cheeses are produced using the supply of local milk in Western New York.

AMERICAN CHEESES

Having identified the main cheese producers in New York State, we analyze what are the various types of cheeses in the United States of America.

- **Specialty Cheese**: cheese limited production to which particular attention is paid to the flavor. They are made with all kinds of milk and can include flavorings such as herbs, spices, fruits and nuts;
- **Artisanal Cheese**: cheeses made by hand, in small quantities and with special attention to tradition. They are made with different kind of milk, and may include flavorings;
- **Farmstead Cheese**: cheeses made in the farm with farmer's milk. The milk used in the production of these cheeses cannot come from the outside the farm. They are made with all types of milk and they may include flavorings.

Below is a brief guide to the various categories of cheeses:

- **Fresh Cheeses**: Mascarpone, Ricotta, Chevre, Feta, Cream Cheese, Quark and Cottage Cheese;
- **Soft-Ripened Cheeses**: Brie and Camembert;
- **Semi-soft Cheeses**: Blue Cheeses, Colby, Fontina, Havarti and Monterey Jack;
- **Firm/Hard Cheeses**: Gouda, Cheddar, Dry Jack, Emmenthaler, Gruyere and Parmesan;
- **Blue Cheeses**: Roquefort and Gorgonzola;

- **Pasta Filata Cheese**: Mozzarella, Provolone and Scamorza;
- **Natural Rind Cheeses**: Tomme de Savoie, Mimolette, Stilton and Lancashire cheese;
- **Washed Rind Cheeses**: Epoisses cheese, Livarot and Taleggio;
- **Processed Cheeses**: American cheese.

Quality of Product: Skim milk for processing has to be manufactured in plants approved by the Agricultural Marketing Service (AMS) Dairy Grading Program.

LAW AND REGULATIONS

The United States of America is a federal state in which each state has its own laws. We focus on the regulations of New York State.

Pasteurization and curing laws and regulations for natural cheeses

Minimum curing time required for most varieties made from unpasteurized milk is 60 days.

Varieties for which longer curing time is required are: Asiago medium (6 months), Asiago old (1 year), Caciocavallo Siciliano (90 days), Gorgonzola (90 days), Gruyere (90 days), Parmesan Reggiano (14 months), Romano (5 months), Sap sago (5 months), Hard Grating (6 months).

Varieties for which pasteurization of milk is required: Muenster, Monterey, High-moisture jack, Neufchatel, Cream, Mozzarella.

Labeling laws and regulations for natural cheeses: bulk

General requirements applicable to all cheese:

- Name of product, name and address of manufacturer or distributor, net weight of contents;
- Applicable only to cheese moving into interstate commerce;

- State brand cheese to be marked with stamp obtained from commissioner;
- Factory number.

Additional labeling applicable only to cheese made from unpasteurized milk:

- Date of manufacture or in lieu thereof be marked or labeled: "Aged 60 days or more". Cheese held longer may show longer period.

Additional labeling applicable only to cheese made from pasteurized milk:

- "Pasteurized".

Labeling laws and regulations for natural cheeses: prepackaged (cut and wrapped)

At plant, warehouse or distributor's establishment for sale at wholesale and retail:

- Name of product, name and address of manufacturer or distributor, net weight of contents;
- Applicable only to cheese moving into interstate commerce;
- The following cheeses in the form of slices or cuts in consumer-sized packages may contain no more than 0.2 percent by weight of sorbic acid, and if the cheese contains sorbic acid it shall be labeled "Sorbic acid added to retard mold growth" or "Sorbic acid added as preservative": Cheddar, Washed curd, Colby, Granular, Swiss, Emmentaler, Gruyere, Brick, Muenster, Edam, Gouda, Monterey, High moisture jack, Provolone, Caciocavallo, Asiago fresh, Semisoft, Semisoft part-skim, Spiced and Part-skim spiced;

Also same as bulk as to pasteurization and aging.

On premises where sold at retail:

- Name of product, name and address of manufacturer or distributor, net weight of contents;

Also same as bulk as to pasteurization and aging.

Composition standards for various natural cheeses

	Milkfat in solids (Min %)	Milkfat (Min %)	Moisture (Max %)
Asiago cheese fresh	50,0		45,0
Asiago cheese medium	45,0		35,0
Asiago cheese old	42,0		32,0
Blue cheese	50,0		46,0
Brick cheese	50,0		44,0
Caciocavallo siciliano cheese	42,0		40,0
Camembert cheese			
Cheddar cheese	50,0		39,0
Colby cheese	50,0		40,0
Cook cheese			80,0
Cream cheese		33,0	55,0
Edam cheese	40,0		45,0
Gammelost cheese			52,0
Gorgonzola cheese	50,0		42,0
Gouda cheese	46,0		45,0
Granular cheese	50,0		39,0
Gruyere cheese	45,0		39,0
Hard cheese	50,0		39,0
Hard grating cheese	32,0		34,0
High Moisture Jack cheese	50,0		>44,0 (Min %); 50,0 (Max %)
Limburger cheese	50,0		50,0
Monterey cheese	50,0		44,0
Munster cheese	50,0		46,0
Pineapple cheese			
Neufchatel cheese		20,0 (Min %);	65,0

		<33,0 (Max %)	
Parmesan cheese	32,0		32,0
Provolone cheese	45,0		45,0
Romano cheese	38,0		34,0
Roquefort cheese	50,0		45,0
Sap sago cheese			38,0
Swiss cheese	43,0		41,0
Semisoft cheese	50,0		>39,0 (Min %); 50,0 (Max %)
Part-skim cheddar cheese			
Part-skim spiced cheese	20,0 (Min %); <50,0 (Max %)		
Semisoft part-skim cheese	45,0 (Min %); <50,0 (Max %)		50,0
Skim milk cheese			
Soft ripened cheese	50,0		
Spiced cheese	50,0		
Washed curd cheese	50,0		42,0
Medium Skim Milk cheese		13,0	
Special skim milk cheese		18,0	
Mozzarella (or Scamorza) brined		18,0	>52,0 (Min %); 58,0 (Max %)
Mozzarella (or Scamorza) unbrined, if sold at retail within 24 hours after its manufacture		16,0	65,0

Part-skim Mozzarella (or Part-skim Scamorza) brined		13,0 (Min %); <18,0 (Max %)	>52,0 (Min %); 60,0 (Max %)
Nuworld cheese	50,0		46,0
Samsoe cheese	45,0		41,0

CONCLUSION

I can suppose that Nonno Nanni has three different solutions to enter the American market. They can first export the product directly from Italy to New-York state. The product will took the plane from Italy to New York's International airport John F. Kennedy that is well connected with Italian flights. However, as it is a fresh product, the transport's conditions should be extremely controlled. The cheese should be transported in fresh compartments in the way that the product should stay the same from the Italian factory to the American shop. This will require high transportation costs because it has to be quick and made in specific conditions.

Secondly, Nonno Nanni can set its own factory on the American territory. It will allow them to be closer to the retailers and so to the consumers. This option will force them to learn the expertise to Americans workers who have no idea of how this cheese is made. This will take time and money to train the workers. They will also have to be able to find the same milk so the same cows as they can have in Italy, which made the quality of the cheese. It can depends on the field, weather; the different raw materials that they can have in Italy are maybe not the same in the US. Before setting the production in the US, they should know if they would be able to reproduce the same product as in Italy. This solution will take time and will cost them a lot.

The third solution will be to set a joint venture with a local

American producer of cheese. Nonno Nanni will not need to invest in a new factory in the US but will just have to train the Americans' workers for them to be able to produce the exact stracchino the same as the Italian's one. If they choose this solution, the company has to be careful that US producers will not become the first competitors of Nonno Nanni so this it is a risk the company will take.

As I know, the company and stracchino is not present yet in the US. There is not direct competitors. As I noticed, Stracchino can have a similar taste with cream cheese, which is present in the US with the brand Philadelphia. This brand belongs to the large group Kraft Foods, which remains the leader in the cheese market in America with 31% market shares. If Nonno Nanni wants to compete by setting the production directly in the US, the company can have difficulties to enter such as small economies of scale because of the small size of the business and a small volume of production at the beginning. They will also need a large amount to invest and maybe they are not able to bring it. They may have to face with governments standards and duty taxes. Nonno Nanni will also need a permitting requirement and a license to establish the production in America. They will have to establish a strong brand identity, as they are not already present on the market because some Americans may prefer to switch to a brand or a product they already know instead of a product they do not trust. This is why Nonno Nanni has to be credible and highlight the "made in Italy" aspect of its product.

REFERENCES

- Planetscope database website: http://www.plantscope.nl/
- Cheesemonger Invitational website: http://www.cheesemongerinvitational.com/
- Statista database website: http://www.statista.com/
- National Dairy Council website: http://www.nationaldairycouncil.org
- American Cheese Society website: www.cheesesociety.org
- "A summary of law and regulations affecting the cheese industry", US Department of Agriculture
- http://finanza-mercati.ilsole24ore.com/quotazioni.php?QUOTE=!EURUS.FX
- http://it.global-rates.com/statistiche-economiche/inflazione/indice-dei-prezzi-al-consumo/cpi/stati-uniti.aspx
- http://www.ilsole24ore.com/art/notizie/2014-10-04/usa-boom-occupazione-081204.shtml?uuid=ABFoqwzB
- https://www.justlanded.com/italiano/Stati-Uniti/Guida-Stati-Uniti/Istruzione/L-educazione-universitaria
- http://www.usda.gov/wps/portal/usda/usdahome
- http://www.battelle.org/docs/tpp/2014_global_rd_funding_forecast.pdf
- http://www.fda.gov/
- http://www.greenproductionguide.com/

www.ingramcontent.com/pod-product-compliance
Lightning Source LLC
Chambersburg PA
CBHW071130220526
45467CB00004B/2124